This robin hides its nest in a bush.

An owl will hide its nest in a tree.

woodpecker

A woodpecker will hide its nest in a tree, too.

A stork hides its nest high up.

This bird hides its nest high up, as well.

A swan hides its nest by the water.

water

This bird will hide its nest by the water, too.

Can you see what a bird hides in its nest?